ORIGAMI NOTE CARDS

FLORENCE TEMKO

TUTTLE PUBLISHING
Tokyo • Rutland, Vermont • Singapore

Published by Tuttle Publishing, an imprint of Periplus Editions (HK) Ltd., with editorial offices at 364 Innovation Drive, North Clarendon, Vermont 05759 U.S.A..

Library of Congress Cataloging-in-Publication Data
Temko, Florence.
  Origami note cards / Florence Temko.
      p. cm.
  ISBN 978-0-8048-3880-1 (pbk.)
1. Origami. 2. Greeting cards. I. Title.
  TT870.T4463 2008
  736'.982—dc22

                                    2007009551

ISBN-10: 0-8048-3880-1
ISBN-13: 978-0-8048-3880-1

Diagrams by Masturah Jeffrey based on original diagrams by Florence Temko

Distributed by

North America, Latin America & Europe
Tuttle Publishing
364 Innovation Drive
North Clarendon, VT 05759-9436 U.S.A.
Tel: 1 (802) 773-8930
Fax: 1 (802) 773-6993
info@tuttlepublishing.com
www.tuttlepublishing.com

Asia Pacific
Berkeley Books Pte. Ltd.
61 Tai Seng Avenue #02-12
Singapore 534167
Tel: (65) 6280-1330
Fax: (65) 6280-6290
inquiries@periplus.com.sg
www.periplus.com

First edition
11 10 09 08   10 9 8 7 6 5 4 3 2

Printed in Hong Kong

CONTENTS

PROJECTS

INTRODUCTION

Anyone receiving a note folded up in a mysterious way will get an extra lift of anticipation. *Origami Note Cards* shows how to fold paper into all kinds of different shapes. Instead of searching for a printed greeting card at a store, you may have fun spending a few minutes folding a piece of ordinary paper into a very personal message to a family member or friend. Even in this electronic age, sending a colorful card is still a popular way to communicate and show that you care.

Over the years I have collected hundreds of patterns for folded notes from all over the world and have selected some of my favorite designs for inclusion in *Origami Note Cards*. You can use them as greetings for birthdays and holidays, invitations, or notes of appreciation. Most patterns can be interchanged to suit any occasion and personalized with colorful papers and added decorations. Many of them are suited for gluing into a scrapbook.

The patterns range from very simple, needing only four or five creases, to more challenging ones. You will also find an unusual way to wrap a few of your handmade note cards, if you decide to give them as presents.

Share the pleasure of making cards with family members of any age, or scouting and other groups. You can even use your cards for fund raising purposes. They can be made ahead of time, ready for future use.

Many school systems now incorporate origami in their curricula, because hands-on activities are beneficial in presenting educational values in reading and math classes and for increasing tactile facility. With creative projects like the ones included in *Origami Note Cards,* students can learn while having fun. And I hope you will too.

Traditions of Folded Cards

Before envelopes were in common use, messages were written on pieces of paper and folded up. The address was written on the outside. Letter writers aimed to lock the paper in such a way that glue or sealing wax was not required.

Envelopes became popular in the mid-nineteenth century when the English post office began to assess mailings by weight and it became cheaper to send

several sheets in one envelope. Previously postage was assessed by the number of sheets sent.

Birthday, Christmas cards, and Valentines were the most popular printed greeting cards until the latter part of the twentieth century, when cards were sent not only to honor special occasions but to keep in touch and as signs of friendship.

In Japan elaborate cards are attached to all gifts and may be shaped into appropriate symbols. For example, cards can be folded to resemble the crane, a long-legged bird with large wings that represents longevity because of its long life span. The elaborateness of a design is a sign of respect afforded to the recipient. Some of the letterfolds in *Origami Note Cards* are based on these designs.

Many people enjoy the creative fun of folding a note into an unusual shape, knowing that the recipient will have a surprise when it is opened.

The History of Origami

"Origami" is a Japanese word consisting of *ori* meaning to fold, and *gami* meaning paper. The word has slipped into the English language because paper-folding has spread from Japan, where it is part of the culture. It is known that since the twelfth century paper has been folded in Japan for ceremonial purposes and that in the sixteenth century paper was folded for decorative use and entertainment.

Records show that paper was folded in Europe in the fourteenth century. In the sixteenth and seventeenth centuries it was common practice to fold square baptismal certificates in set patterns and keep them in the family Bible.

The kind of recreational origami now popular in Asia and Western countries began in the late nineteenth century, but received its greatest impetus in the latter half of the twentieth century. Now origami clubs exist in many countries. Members of all ages meet to exchange directions for models and share other information. It's great fun to meet other paper-folders at these gatherings, which are very welcoming to anyone of any age. In addition annual international conventions take place in many localities. The annual convention in New York City sponsored

by OrigamiUSA attracts more than 600 enthusiasts from all over the world.

Many paperfolders like to follow the instructions provided by others, but some like to create their own designs. Today's most prolific creators seem to have a mathematical, scientific, or artistic inclination of which they may not even be aware. Akira Yoshizawa of Japan is considered the master of artistic origami designs, which are much admired. His animals seem to come alive, poised ready to run or jump.

Dr. Robert Lang, an American scientist, is intrigued by the challenge of devising insects that duplicate their natural details. Some creations by these and other masters have become well recognized as works of art. They have been displayed in major art museums and sold in art galleries. Some may require only a few creases while others may be made with hundreds—yes, hundreds—of steps.

Dr. Lang has devised the Treemaker software, which bases folding patterns on proportions of the location and size of points on the surface of the paper. Erik Demaine, a young professor at the Massachusetts Institute of Technology, explores the mathematics behind origami. Both he and Robert Lang are deeply involved in adapting origami techniques to scientific purposes in the auto industry, space exploration, and other areas.

You can satisfy your curiosity about any aspect of Origami on the Internet, where it is well represented. Traditional and new designs, whether simple or complex, appear constantly on Web sites.

ABOUT ORIGAMI TECHNIQUES

To help you make sense of the lines and arrows on the diagrams, it will be well worth your while to take a few minutes to study the explanations of some basic techniques. Learn to recognize the following procedures, which are international standards for origami.

1. Valley Fold

Folding the paper toward you is called a valley fold and is shown by a line of dashes in the diagrams.

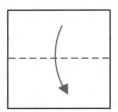

a.

b.

a. Fold the square in half toward you, matching it to the opposite edge.
b. You have made a valley fold.

2. Mountain Fold

Folding paper to the back, away from you, is called a mountain fold and is shown by a line of dashes and dots in the diagrams.

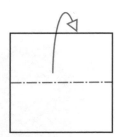

a.

b.

a. Fold the square in half by guiding the paper to the *back,* matching it to the opposite edge.
b. You have made a mountain fold.

3. Existing Crease

A crease made previously is shown in the diagrams by a thin line that does not touch the edges.

4. Arrows

In the diagrams you will see four kinds of arrows. They indicate the direction in which to fold.

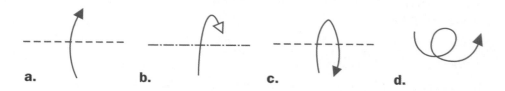

a. Make a valley fold.
b. Make a mountain fold.
c. Double Arrow—fold and unfold the same crease.
d. Curly Arrow—turn the paper over.

Helpful Tips

These tips will alert you to common problems you may encounter. If you are having trouble with any step, always check the following:

1. Make sure you distinguish carefully between a valley fold (dashed line) and a mountain fold (dash-dot-dash line).
2. Be sure to observe the curly arrow asking you to turn the paper over.
3. Compare your paper to the illustrations for
    the step you are working on;
    the step before; and
    the next one, which is your goal.
4. Read the directions out loud.

Diagrams

On all diagrams action to be taken is shown in red. Darker shading on the diagrams indicates the colored side of the paper, which is helpful if you are using paper that is colored on only one side, such as origami squares or gift wrap.

For the sake of clarity, the illustrations may increase in size from the beginning of the project to the end. But the angles are always consistent and you can test your own paper against them.

Measurements

Measurements are given in inches and centimeters, but they may not always be exactly equal, in order to avoid awkward fractions. In some cases specific sizes are recommended, but in most cases you may use smaller or larger pieces of paper.

Degree of Difficulty

On a scale of difficulty the projects vary from simple to intermediate.

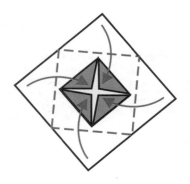
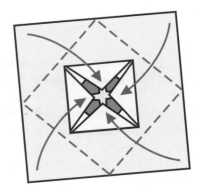
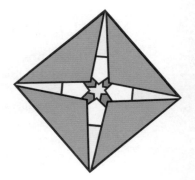

ABOUT PAPER

The paper squares included in this kit are of a typical weight well suited to origami. Origami squares in varying sizes and colors are also available in some art, museum, and gift stores, as well as from catalogs. They are usually colored on one side and white on the other.

Many origami projects require square paper, including some in *Origami Note Cards*. Squares have four sides of equal length and all their corners form right (90°) angles. If you need additional squares, or want to use special papers, you can cut them on a board paper cutter, if available, or follow these easy instructions:

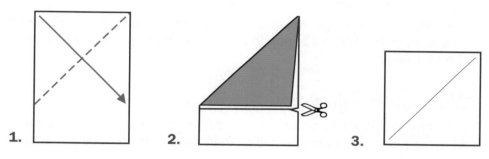

1. Fold a short edge to a long edge.
2. Cut off the extra rectangle.
3. A square.

Copy and other printing papers (8½" x 11") can easily be cut into two sizes:

- With one cut, you will have a square with 8½" sides.
- With two cuts you will have two squares with 5½" sides.

For a small fee copy shops will usually cut a whole ream of 500 sheets, which will provide five hundred 8½" squares or a thousand 5½" squares.

Most fairly thin, uncoated paper with a crisp surface is suitable for origami. When creating your origami note cards, you may also want to experiment with some of the following types of paper.

Letter and Printing Paper

These types of paper are available in a large assortment of colors at copy shops, office supply stores, and school suppliers. They are sold in size 8½" x 11" in packages of 500 sheets (a ream), and are available in two weights described on the package wrapping as 24 lbs and 20 lbs. The lighter weight folds more easily. Printing papers are most economical for schools, youth groups, and other large groups.

When projects work equally well with A4 size paper, it is indicated at the beginning of their instructions.

Gift Wrap Paper

The careful choice of gift wrap paper can add individuality to your origami projects. It is quite difficult to cut paper on rolls to the right size, but well worthwhile for the special results.

Handmade Papers

This type of paper is softer, but gives rich-looking results. Japanese washi paper in glorious patterns is available in sheets or packages of squares.

Recycled Paper

You may find that out-of-date flyers, or colorful magazine pages, can be used for origami.

COPYRIGHT AND DESIGN USE

You may fold any origami and photocopy printed instructions for your own personal use, but you cannot include any instructions in handouts or any printed or electronic format without permission from the creator or copyright holder, which may be a publisher.

There are three sources of origami designs, called models, which influence use and copyright.

- Traditional: In many cultures toys and other things are folded from paper, like the dart airplane or the hat made from a newspaper. These may be used and taught by anyone but printed instructions and diagrams still may not be copied without permission of the creator or publisher.
- Known creators: When paperfolders show or teach models by known creators they always credit them by name. For commercial use permission must be sought from the creator.
- Unknown creators: When a model is handed around informally at parties, in schools and elsewhere, the name of the creator may become lost in the shuffle.

The models that appear in *Origami Note Cards* are either my own designs, created by designers who have been credited, or traditional.

FURTHER INFORMATION

Readers interested in learning more about paperfolding can search for "origami" on the Internet. The following groups can connect you with other paperfolders in your area or your country:

OrigamiUSA
15 West 77th Street
New York, NY 10024
USA
www.origami-usa.org

British Origami Society
c/o Penny Groom
2A The Chestnuts
Countesthorpe, Leicester
LE8 5TL, United Kingdom

ELFA (Envelope and Letterfold Association) is a small group of paperfolders that specializes in letter and envelope folding. They can be contacted at:

ELFA International
Twenge 4
Langenhagen
Germany D30855
www.xs4all.nl/~ploegevd/index.html

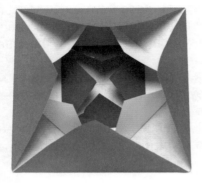

PATRIOTIC CARD

For a national holiday make this card in colors of a specific country. For the Fourth of July I used red, white, and blue paper. For Cinco de Mayo, the Mexican colors of red and green with a white outside square would be appropriate. The card reveals a hidden message when the recipient opens it.

You need:

- 3 pieces of colored printing paper, in red, white, and blue, or other colors of your choice

- Glue

If the paper is colored on only one side, begin with the white side facing up.

From the red paper cut a 6" (15 cm) square.

From the white paper cut a 4" (10 cm) square.

From the blue paper cut a 2¾" (7 cm) square.

Fold all three squares the same way.

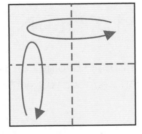

1. Fold the square in half in both directions, unfolding each time.

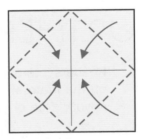

2. Fold the four corners to the center.

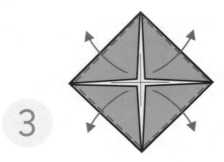

3. Unfold the four corners.

4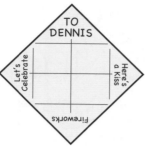

4. Each piece of paper will have four triangles. Write a message on all twelve triangles. Here are some ideas: "To Dennis," "Happy 4th of July," "Fireworks," "Let's celebrate," "Here's a kiss."

6

6a. Glue the folded (blue) square to the inside center of the next larger size (white) paper.

6b. Fold the corners in again.

8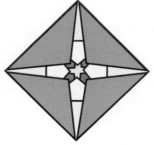

8. Completed *Patriotic Card*.

5

5. On the smallest square (blue) fold the four corners in again.

7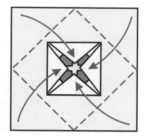

7a. Glue the joined squares to the biggest (red) square.

7b. Fold the corners in again.

Patriotic Ornament

When you leave the card half open it can become a hanging ornament. You only have to attach a loop of thread to one corner. All three colors will be revealed.

The card is also very attractive when made with only white paper.

15

IT'S THE CAT'S MEOW

You can decorate a greeting card with this simple image of a cat, the most popular of all pets. Paper colored the same on both sides works best.

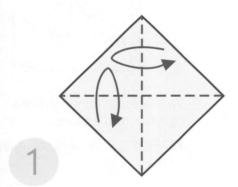

1

1a. Fold the square on both diagonals.

1b. Unfold each time.

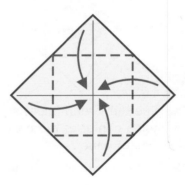

2

2. Fold the four corners to the center.

3

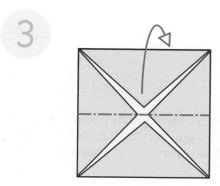

3. Mountain-fold the paper in half, to the BACK.

4

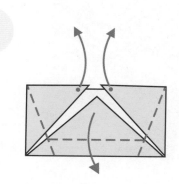

4a. Fold down the corner from the middle.

4b. You will see two triangles on the outer edges. Form the ears by grasping the original corners of the paper and pulling them straight up.

5

5. Completed *It's the Cat's Meow*.

Surprise Tip

Turn the cat upside down and it will be a dog.

17

FOR MOTHER'S DAY

This note card always elicits appreciative comments for its elegant design. For best effect use fairly light paper and make very sharp creases.

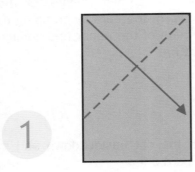

1. Fold the short top edge to the long edge, right through the middle of the right top corner.

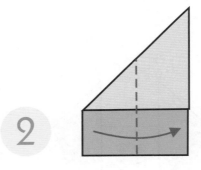

2. Fold the note in half.

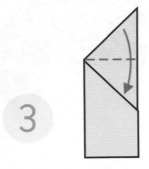

3. Fold down the top corner.

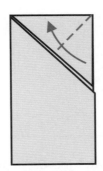

4. On the triangle fold the lower corner over, as shown.

5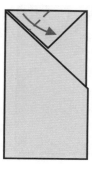

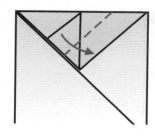

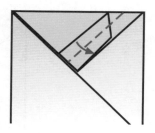

5. Steps 5a to 5c show how to prepare the shaded triangle for accordion pleating like a fan, which will later form a shell.

5a. Fold the loose corner inward, as shown.

5b. Fold over again,

5c. . . . and fold over once more.

6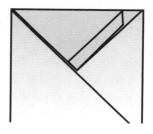

7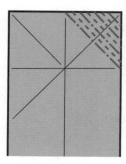

8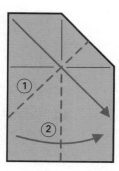

6. Unfold the paper completely.

7. Fan fold on the creases made in step 5, alternating mountain and valley folds by folding one crease up and the next crease down. Begin with the longest crease as a mountain fold.

8. The pleats will be hidden.

Refold steps 1–2.

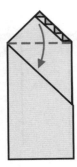

9. Fold down the triangle with the pleats.

 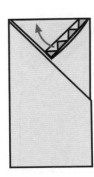

10. Spread the pleats into a shell shape by pushing the left half over and spreading all pleats a little.

11. Completed *For Mother's Day*.

Tips

To help the note keep its shape, weigh it down with a book for a while.

Mailing

The Mother's Day note can be mailed. The shell may get a little flattened, but will survive. Extra postage may be required.

Gift Certificate

Include a coupon for a special treat for Mother, promising her extra help or something else you think she may appreciate.

QUICKIE NOTE

Here's a note that's quick to make and easy to fold.

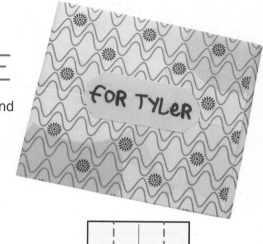

You need:

- A piece of letter paper, 8½" x 11" (or A4)

If the paper is colored on only one side, begin with the white side facing up.

1

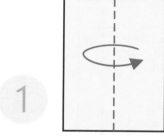

1a. Fold the paper in half the long way.

1b. Unfold the paper flat.

2

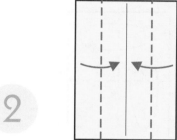

2. Fold the long outside edges to the crease you just made.

3

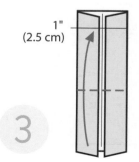

1"
(2.5 cm)

3. Fold up the bottom edge to about an inch (2.5 cm) below the top edge.

4

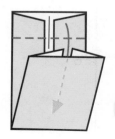

4. Fold down the top and slide it inside the pocket formed in step 3.

5

5. Completed *Quickie Note*.

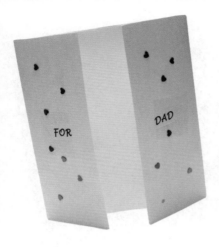

FATHER'S DAY CARD

Tell your Dad how much you love him with this giant card. You can make it in any size, but the B-I-G-G-E-R the better.

You need:

- A very large sheet of stiff paper, ideally 20" x 40" (50 cm x 1 m) for a card 10" x 20" (25 cm x 50 cm)

- A pencil
- Scissors
- Markers

For best results, your paper should be the same color on the front and back and shouldn't be too dark.

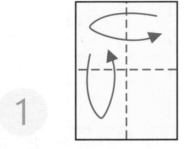

1

1a. Fold the paper in quarters.

1b. Unfold the paper flat.

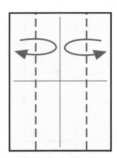

2

2a. Fold the long sides to the middle.

2b. Unfold the paper flat.

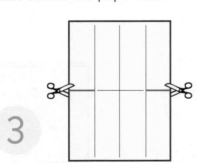

3

3. Cut in from both sides to the nearest creases.

4

4. Draw a picture of yourself. The head and arms must be on the top half. Most of the body should be on the lower half. Inside write: "I love you this much."

5

5. On the upper part fold the side edges to the middle on the creases already made.

6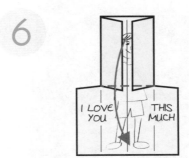

6. Fold the paper in half from top to bottom.

7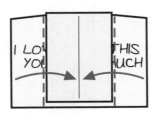

7. Fold the side edges to the middle on the creases already made.

8

8a. On the front write: "For Dad."

8b. Completed *Father's Day Card*.

Tip

Add stickers, photos, or other decorations. Or write a story—begin on the front, open the two sides and write the next part of the story, and finish as the card is opened once more.

IT'S A WRAP

You will find many uses for this simple, yet decorative envelope. You can use it as gift wrap for a few of your handmade cards, or for other flat items, such as a scarf or a tie. When you make it smaller you can glue it into a scrapbook to hide a photo or personal message as a surprise. You can close the envelope with small pieces of velcro, or, for a decorative touch, lock it with a toothpick by following the steps on page 26.

You need:

- A piece of gift wrap, 12" x 24" (30 cm x 60 cm)

- A ruler

- A pencil

- Scissors

If the paper is colored on only one side, begin with the white side facing up.

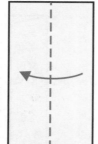

1. Fold the piece in half the long way.

2. Fold the folded piece in half the short way.

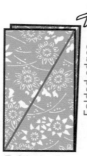

Folded edges

Folded edge

3a. Place the paper exactly as shown, with the folded edges on the right and at the bottom.

3b. Draw a line from the top right corner to the bottom left corner and cut on it through all layers.

4

4. Unfold the paper flat.

5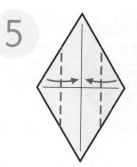

5. You will have a diamond. Fold both side corners to the middle crease.

6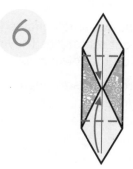

6. Fold the top and bottom corners toward the middle. Note that the creases start a little way in from the folded edges.

7

7. Completed *It's a Wrap*. (See next page for how to seal this project.)

closure

You can close the envelope with small pieces of velcro, or, for a decorative touch, lock it with a toothpick by following these three steps.

1. On the top flap cut out a small rectangle, about 1 in (3 cm) up from the pointed corner.

2a. Place the top flap (not shown) on the lower flap.

2b. Mark two small circles inside the cut-out rectangle. They will appear on the lower flap.

2c. Pierce holes through the two small circles.

3. Lock the envelope by inserting a toothpick through the two small holes that show up inside the rectangle. Slide the toothpick into the little right hole, then under and out through the left hole.

JOURNAL BOOK

This little book is a convenient way to share your thoughts or photos with someone who may be far away or just around the corner. This book is a very popular project for scrapbooking and other purposes, because it is simple, yet effective.

You need:

- A piece of letter paper, 8½" x 11" (or A4)

- A piece of paper 4¼" x 22" (11 cm x 60 cm)

If the letter paper is colored on only one side, begin with the white side facing up. The other piece of paper should be a color light enough to write on.

cover

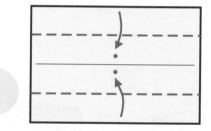

1a. Fold the letter paper in half the long way. Unfold it.

1b. Fold the long edges to the crease, but leave a small gap in between, about ¼" (½ cm).

GAP

2a. Fold the paper in half the short way. Unfold it.

2b. Fold the short edges to the crease, but again leave a small gap in between.

3. Completed cover.

pages

1

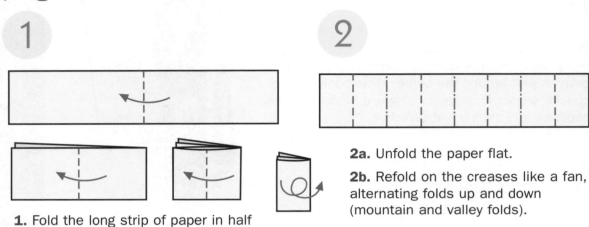

1. Fold the long strip of paper in half three times.

2

2a. Unfold the paper flat.

2b. Refold on the creases like a fan, alternating folds up and down (mountain and valley folds).

assembly

1

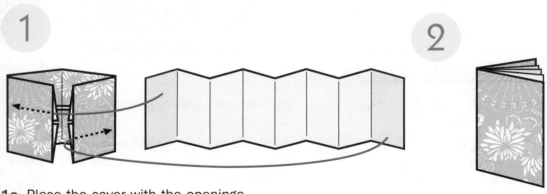

1a. Place the cover with the openings facing you.

1b. Place the pleated pages with the ends of the paper facing up, toward you.

1c. Slide the first and last pages into the pockets on the cover.

2

2. Completed *Journal Book*.

Tips

You can avoid having to deal with precise measurements for producing the long strip by cutting a piece of letter paper in half the long way. Then affix the two short ends together with tape.

Sizes

The given dimensions were chosen to take advantage of standard sizes of letter paper, and will result in a book 3" x 4¼" (7 cm x 11 cm), but books can be made in other sizes, keeping the same proportions.

For a smaller book, size 1½" x 2¼" (4 cm x 6 cm), use paper:

  4" x 6" (10 cm x 15 cm) for the cover
  2" x 12" (5 cm x 30 cm) for the inside pages

For a bigger book, size 6" x 8" (15 cm x 20 cm), use paper:

  16" x 24" (40 cm x 60 cm) for the cover
  8" x 48" (20 cm x 120 cm) for the inside pages

HAVE A GOOD TRIP!

Sometimes you may want to express good wishes to someone going on a trip. Whether for a cruise or an airplane or car trip, the origami sailboat says: "Sail into a wonderful time!"

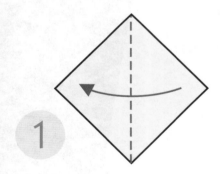

1. Fold the square from corner to corner.

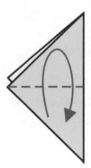

2. Fold the the triangle in half and unfold it.

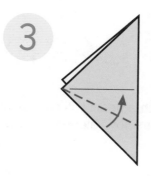

3. Fold the lower slanted edge to lie along the crease made in step 2. See the next diagram.

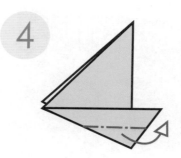

4. Mountain-fold the bottom corner under, to the back.

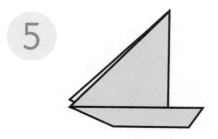

5. Completed *Have a Good Trip!*

Tip

You can fold this sailboat from squares of various sizes. Try gluing them on blank greeting cards, nametags, or placecards.

HEART CARD

A card decorated with a heart will convey your love and good wishes for Valentine's Day or any other occasion.

You need:

- A red paper square with 5" (12 cm) sides

- A 5" x 7" (A5) blank greeting card, or a rectangle of sturdy paper folded in half

- Glue stick

If paper is colored only on one side, begin with the white side facing up.

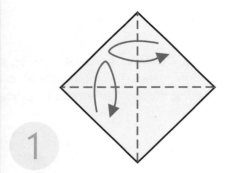

1. Fold the square from corner to corner in both directions, unfolding the paper flat each time.

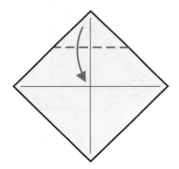

2. Fold the top corner to the center where the creases meet.

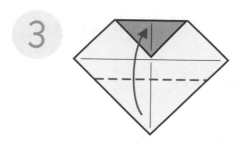

3. Fold the bottom corner to the top edge.

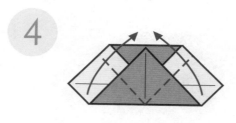

4. Fold both sides at an angle to the middle crease.

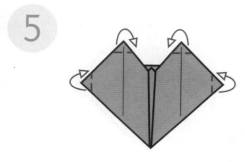

5. Mountain-fold the two top corners and the two side corners to the back.

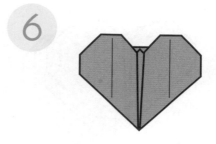

6. Completed *Heart*. Glue it to the front of a blank greeting card.

Pop - Up

If you glue down only the lower part of the heart, it will become somewhat three-dimensional.

HEARTS AND FLOWERS

This is a bonus project, because it uses the same heart you already learned to fold. This time you fold four smaller hearts and combine them into a flower.

You need:

- 4 red paper squares with 2½" (7 cm) sides

- A green paper square with 2½" (7 cm) sides

- A blank 5" x 7" (A5) greeting card, or a rectangle of sturdy paper folded in half

- Glue stick

If the green paper for the leaf is colored only on one side, place the colored side facing up.

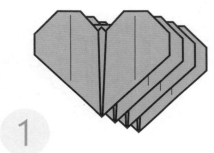

1

1. Use the Heart Card instructions to fold the four red squares into hearts. Put them aside.

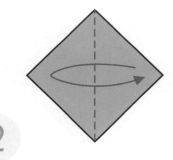

2

2a. Fold the square from corner to corner.

2b. Unfold the paper flat.

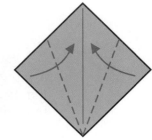

3

3. Fold two side edges to the crease.

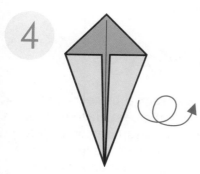

4. Turn the paper over.

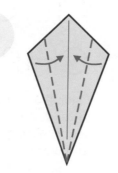

5. Fold the two long side edges to the crease.

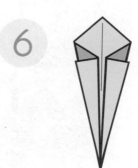

6. Reach behind and swing the hidden corners out to the sides.

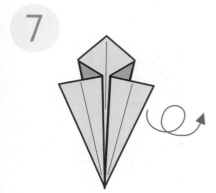

7. Turn the paper over.

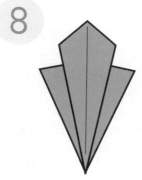

8. Completed leaf. Glue the hearts and the leaf on a blank greeting card.

9. Completed *Hearts and Flowers.*

MERRY CHRISTMAS

Fold this Christmas tree from a piece of green letter or printing paper. For the best placement of your greeting, fold the Christmas tree completely and unfold it; then write your message in the central space before refolding the model. You can also glue the tree to a blank greeting card.

1a. Fold the short bottom edge to the long edge making the crease through the left bottom corner.

1b. Unfold the paper flat.

2a. Fold the short edge to the opposite long edge, making the crease through the right bottom corner.

2b. Unfold the paper flat.

3. You will see an X on the paper. Mountain-fold to the BACK right through middle of the X.

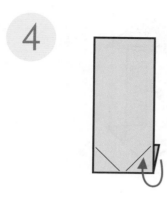

4. Flip the back layer to the front, loosely.

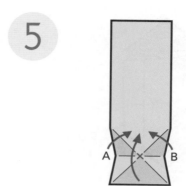

5. Push down on the middle of the X. Then grasp both sides of the paper and bring A and B together in the middle. Flatten the top of the paper into a triangle. See the next diagram.

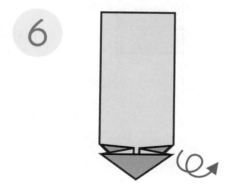

6. Turn the paper over.

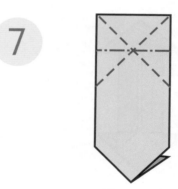

7. Repeat steps 1 through 5 at the opposite end of the paper.

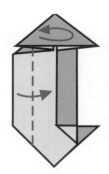

8. Gently lift up the right corner of the triangle to the left, but do not crease. This will permit you to fold the right edge to the middle. Then guide the triangle back to its previous position. See the next diagram.

9. Repeat step 8 on the left side.

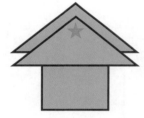

11. Completed *Merry Christmas*.

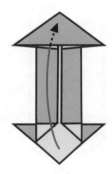

10. Grasp the bottom corner of the paper and roll it behind the top layer of the triangle at the top. Make a sharp crease when the bottom edges of the triangles are about ½" (1 cm) apart.

Tip

You can make a bigger tree from gift wrap. Glue two pieces of gift wrap back to back so that the pattern shows up on the back and the front. Then cut it to size 6" x 15" (15 cm x 40 cm).

KWANZAA KALEIDOSCOPE

Kwanzaa is an annual celebration held from December 26 to January 1, honoring African-American heritage. On each day emphasis is placed on a different value, such as unity and creativity. This kaleidoscope card, made up of a group of interlocking origami triangles, is a perfect representation of unity. Red, green, and black are traditional Kwanzaa colors. You can also create your own designs with different colors and patterns.

You need:

- 8 paper squares with 2½" (6 cm) sides
- Glue
- A blank 5" x 7" (A5) greeting card, or a rectangle of sturdy paper folded in half

If the paper is colored on only one side, begin with the colored side facing up.

Fold all eight squares in the same way.

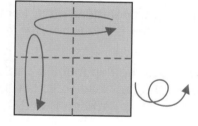

1

1a. Fold the square in half both ways. Unfold the paper flat each time.

1b. Turn the paper over.

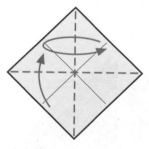

2

2a. Fold the square from corner to corner. Unfold the paper flat.

2b. Fold the square from corner to corner in the other direction, but leave it folded. You will have a triangle.

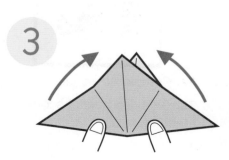

3

3. Grasp the paper with both hands at the folded edge in the exact position shown. Move your hands toward each other until the paper forms another triangle. Place it flat on the table.

4

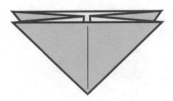

4a. Make sure the triangle has two flaps on each side. If you have only one flap on one side and three on the other, flip one flap over.

4b. Completed Kaleidoscope unit.

2

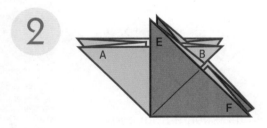

2a. Two units assembled. Glue them together.

2b. Interlock the other six units in the same way.

1 assembly

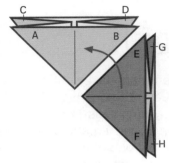

1a. Place two units next to each other, one horizontal and the other vertical.

In the diagram the front flaps of the horizontal triangle are labeled A and B. The back flaps are labeled C and D.

On the vertical triangle the front flaps are labelled E and F, and the back flaps G and H.

1b. Move the flap marked E to lie on top of the flap marked B. Let the flap marked G lie between B and D.

3

3a. Completed Kaleidoscope.

3b. Glue the Kaleidoscope on a blank greeting card.

3c. Completed *Kwanzaa Kaleidoscope*.

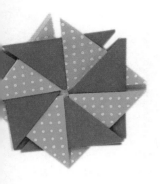

Tips

Papers

The medallion may also be sent flat in an envelope. When it is opened, surprisingly, it pops into three dimensions. You may also find that you can enhance a scrapbook layout with one or more units.

The instructions show how to use eight squares of printing paper in two different colors. Squares may also be cut from patterned gift wrap, but this can be tedious, as all pieces must have the exact same design. It's easier to find suitable papers on the Internet by searching for information about teabag folding. Several sites offer free designs.

Teabag Folding

The term originated in the Netherlands, where envelopes for teabags are printed in attractive patterns. One day, when Tiny van der Plaas needed a greeting card, she resorted to using these envelopes to form a medallion. In time her idea developed into a hobby for many people, who have developed other origami folds to create different patterns.

Geometric Folding

Kaleidoscope origami is an excellent example of circular symmetry.

Every evening during the eight-day Jewish celebration of Hanukkah candles are placed into a candleholder called a menorah. Fold this candle from two pieces of colored paper and send as a holiday greeting.

for the flame

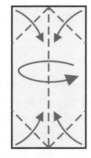

1a. Fold the orange paper in half the long way, and unfold it.

1b. Fold all four corners to the crease.

2. Fold the four slanted edges to the middle crease.

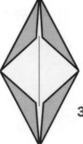

3. Completed Flame (back).

for the candle

 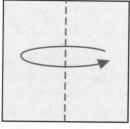

1. Fold the blue paper in half the long way, and unfold it.

 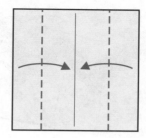

2. Fold the two side edges to the crease.

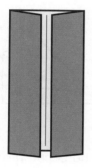

3. Completed Candle (back).

assembly

 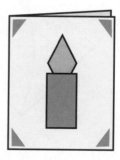

1a. Slide the flame into the candle and glue them to a greeting card.

1b. Completed *Hanukkah Greeting*.

CLASSIC JAPANESE CARD

You can use this design as a greeting card by writing your message inside or on a separate piece of paper you can insert into the card. You can also use it as a wallet or as a gift wrap for a small flat gift.

Using a square of gift wrap paper with a small pattern will create a very pleasing effect. A 10" (25 cm) square will result in a 5" (12 cm) card.

You need:

• A paper square

If the paper is colored on only one side, begin with the white side facing up.

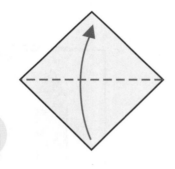

1

1. Fold the square from corner to corner.

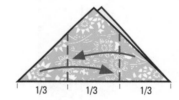

2

2a. Fold the paper into thirds; first the right corner over to the left.

2b. Then the left corner to the right.

3

3. Fold the right corner over to the left.

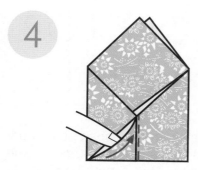

4. Poke your finger into the pocket formed by the double layers of paper and separate them to form a square. See the next diagram.

5. Slide the top corners into the square pocket which you just formed.

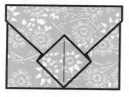

6. Completed *Classic Japanese Card*.

Two-Tone Card

The two-tone version shown in the photograph was made with two squares of thin handmade Japanese washi paper. One square is cut ½" (1 cm) smaller than the other. With colored sides on both squares facing up, glue both pieces together, leaving a border all around.

ENVELOPE FOR ANY NOTE

You may want to match an envelope to the paper used in one of your origami note cards, or you may need an odd size. This simple envelope is folded from a square of gift wrap paper. The given size will produce an envelope about 7" x 6" (18 cm x 14 cm). You can make different sizes from squares in other sizes to suit your needs.

You need:

- A 10" (25 cm) paper square
- Glue or tape

If the paper is colored only on one side, begin with the white side facing up.

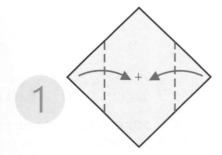

1a. Find the center of the paper by bringing one corner to the opposite corner; do not crease the paper but make only a small nick or light pencil mark.

1b. Fold two opposite corners to the mark.

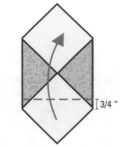

2. Fold the bottom corner up, taking in about ¾" (1½" cm) of the folded edges.

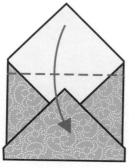

3. Fold the top down taking in about ¾" (1½" cm) of the folded edges.

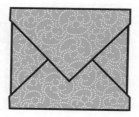

4a. Glue the overlapping parts of the envelope or seal them with tape.

4b. Completed *Envelope for Any Note.*

Tip

This envelope can be sent through the mail when you observe the limits set by the Postal Service. The address will show up better on paper in light colors or the address can be affixed on a label.

ACKNOWLEDGMENTS

Big and heartfelt thanks to my family (Yolanda, Tyler, Janet, Dennis, David, Perri, and Rachel), and my friends and neighbors, for supporting me throughout the writing of *Origami Note Cards*. I wish I could thank everyone individually, but would like to express my special appreciation to John Cunliffe and Elsje van der Ploeg of ELFA, the International Envelope and Letter Folding Association; and to Amanda Dupuis, my editor.